Being Responsible

A Book About Responsibility

by Mary Small   illustrated by Stacey Previn

PICTURE WINDOW BOOKS
Minneapolis, Minnesota

Thanks to our advisors for their expertise, research, and advice:

Bambi L. Wagner, Director of Education
Institute for Character Development, Des Moines, Iowa
National Faculty Member/ Trainer,
Josephson Institute of Ethics - CHARACTER COUNTS!℠
Los Angeles, California

Susan Kesselring, M.A., Literacy Educator
Rosemount-Apple Valley-Egan (Minnesota) School District

Editorial Director: Carol Jones
Managing Editor: Catherine Neitge
Creative Director: Keith Griffin
Editor: Jacqueline A. Wolfe
Story Consultant: Terry Flaherty
Designer: Joe Anderson
Page Production: Picture Window Books
The illustrations in this book were created with acrylics.

Picture Window Books
5115 Excelsior Boulevard
Suite 232
Minneapolis, MN 55416
877-845-8392
www.picturewindowbooks.com

Printed in the United States of America.

Library of Congress Cataloging-in-Publication Data
Small, Mary.
Being responsible / by Mary Small ; illustrated by Stacey Previn.
p. cm. – (Way to be!)
Includes bibliographical references and index.
ISBN 1-4048-1052-8 (hardcover)
1. Responsibility–Juvenile literature. I. Previn, Stacey. II. Title. III. Series.
BJ1451.S62 2006
179'.9–dc22   2005004275

Responsibility is a big word

for something we do every day. Being responsible means doing the things you are supposed to do.

No one else can do your homework or chores for you. No one else can tell the truth for you. These are things only you can do by yourself. When you do what you are supposed to do, you are being responsible.

There are lots of ways to show you are responsible.

John avoids a mud puddle because
he is wearing his dress clothes.

John is being responsible.

The family hurries in the morning to make sure they get to Grandma's on time.

They are being responsible.

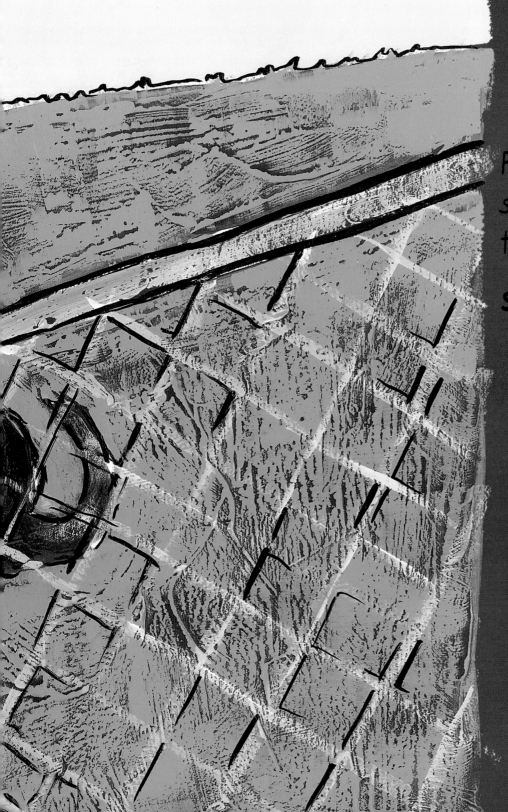

Patricia carefully locks the gate so her dog will stay safely in the yard.

She is being responsible.

Patricia cleans up after her dog when they are taking a walk or playing in the park.

She is being responsible.

Kelly and her brothers quickly rush to get ready so they can catch the bus in time.

They are being responsible.

Even though it is raining,
Angie helps her little brother cross the
street safely.

She is being responsible.

Bridget wears a helmet when riding her bike.

She is being responsible.

Zach feeds his animals on time.

He is being responsible.

Adam carefully brushes his teeth every morning and night.

He is being responsible.

Jaime returns her library books on time.

She is being responsible.

At the Library

Loewen, Nancy. *Do I Have To? : Kids Talk About Responsibility.* Minneapolis: Picture Window Books, 2003.

Rose, Gill. *William and the Guinea Pig.* Minneapolis: Picture Window Books, 2005.

Schuette, Sarah L. *I am Responsible.* Mankato, Minn.: Pebble Books, 2003.

On the Web

FactHound offers a safe, fun way to find Web sites related to this book.

All of the sites on FactHound have been researched by our staff.

www.facthound.com

1. Visit the FactHound home page.
2. Enter a search word related to this book, or type in this special code: 1404810528
3. Click the FETCH IT button.

Your trusty FactHound will fetch the best Web sites for you!

Index

Look for all of the books in the Way to Be! series:

Being Fair: A Book About Fairness

Being a Good Citizen: A Book About Citizenship

Being Respectful: A Book About Respectfulness

Being Responsible: A Book About Responsibility

Being Trustworthy: A Book About Trustworthiness

Caring: A Book About Caring